For Betty and Denys,
who brought me up after I was abandoned by wolves

FIRST PEEL THE OTTER

JOHN HENRY DIXON

WITH ILLUSTRATIONS BY
SPARKS

ABSOLUTE PRESS

FIRST, PEEL THE OTTER

FIRST PUBLISHED IN GREAT BRITAIN
IN THE YEAR MMIV BY

ABSOLUTE PRESS,
PUBLISHERS OF
SCARBOROUGH HOUSE
29 JAMES STREET WEST
BATH BA1 2BT ENGLAND
TELEPHONE
+44 (0) 1225 316013
FACSIMILE
+44 (0) 1225 445836
ELECTRONIC MAILING ADDRESS
INFO@ABSOLUTEPRESS.CO.UK
VIRTUAL DOMAIN RESIDENCE
WWW.ABSOLUTEPRESS.CO.UK

© **JOHN HENRY DIXON**, MMIV

A CATALOGUE RECORD OF THIS BOOK IS
AVAILABLE FROM THE BRITISH LIBRARY.

INTERNATIONAL STANDARD BOOK NUMBER
1 904573 22 3

PRINTED AND BOUND BY LEGOPRINT, PRINTERS OF ITALY

Contents

A SECOND CHANCE

I suppose it was always inevitable that I should compile what many have been kind enough to refer to as the definitive cookery book of its time. I remember as a small child watching spellbound and open-mouthed as my dear, late, great-aunt Sopwith, ancient Peterson pipe clenched firmly between her teeth, skilfully prepared the most mouth-watering, and sometimes highly secret, recipes for our family's consumption. The seeds were sown there and then and some of her secrets are with me still. That is until now. Secrets they are no longer. At last, after something of a false start, I present them once more, along with many of my own, later, discoveries.

The false start to which I refer, of course, is very much on the public record and remains, if not actually a scandal, certainly a matter of some notoriety. It is still, to me, a painful memory to recall that this book was withdrawn from circulation all those years ago, only three weeks after its original release. My then publisher, an odious man, of whom I intend to say very little here, was clearly blind to the benefits to be gained from new styles of culinary expertise. He was also keen to cultivate and maintain influential and powerful friendships. Claiming that his deputy, acting in his absence, had agreed to publication without the requisite authority, he withdrew *First, Peel the Otter* from circulation immediately on his return from abroad and all copies were burnt. We, of course, now know his true motives. Thus, for example, the ground-breaking menu prepared for the Royal Gala Dinner in honour of Prince Rigor of Catatonia was lost to posterity. This was, for me, a labour of love and the grandest of feasts. It was surely a tragedy that these dishes were never again available to a wider audience.

So, too, the unfortunate incident of the soufflé, the missing kitchen-maid and the Cock in Cider. Sadly, for legal reasons which would otherwise, even now, compromise my liberty, these particular delicacies must remain hidden for ever from the light of day. Happily, however, contained within these pages are many more concoctions that, now free from the constraints engendered by shortages of supply, the bigotry of cowardly editors and the hypocrisy of the Prime Minister of the day, may again be experienced and enjoyed.

It is not often that one is offered a second chance in life, so let us all rejoice that the gruesome, the grim and the ghastly are, once more, before us all.

John Henry Dixon,
The Summer House,
Late August.

I. BEGINNINGS

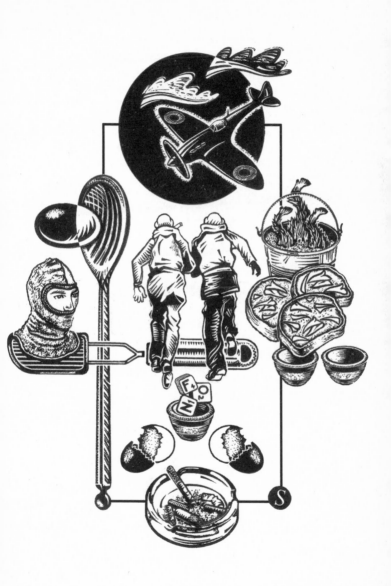

ALPHABET SOUP

1 Scrabble set
2 pts stock

Unpack the board game. Remove the four letter-racks and slice them into quarter-inch Juliennes. Discard the rules and the board, not forgetting the little bag that can be found inside. Place all the letters into a mixing bowl with the stock and stir until you have an insoluble anagram. Serve cold into small bowls, ensuring that no helping scores more than 17. Garnish with the Juliennes.

S¹E¹R¹V⁴E¹S¹ 9

You could follow this with Game Pie – see p72.

ONE TON SOUP

20 cwt lead piping*
83 ground hot chillies
5 lbs turmeric
3 lbs 2 oz ground cumin
1 oz ground coriander
76 garlic cloves (crushed)
2 small onions (chopped)

Melt the lead in a saucepan. Now say something to the lead which will make it really angry and leave it to simmer for half an hour. Add the spices, cloves and onions and cook for a further five minutes. Serve piping hot.

* You could use Dixon's Patent Cooking Lead instead.

CIGARETTE SOUP

20 low-tar cigarettes
1 small glass ashtray
4 drops nicotine essence
1 pt double cream
vegetable oil

gnoring the ill-mannered warnings on the packet, remove the filters from the cigarettes with pile-tweezers and put them aside for later. Peel the cigarettes and place the tobacco in a food processor. If you are watching your weight you may find it useful here to add a disposable lighter. Smash the ashtray under a tea towel with a sledgehammer or the head of a cat and put the pieces into the mixer. Blend until you have a crunchy and sparkly paste. Now slowly add the cream until the mixture has the texture of a small hedgehog. Add the nicotine essence, pour into a bowl and put into the fridge for half an hour. Meanwhile, in a heavy-bottomed pan, heat the oil until very hot and then flash-fry the filters until they are crisp but not burnt. Scatter them over the soup just before serving. It is healthier to leave about half an inch of soup in the bottom of the bowl.

EGGS BENEDICTINE

6 eggs
1 pt holy water
1 cassock
1 incense stick

Break the eggs into a pudding basin, add the holy water and whisk to a theocratic froth. Invert the basin over your head and, using an electric razor, shave off all the hair that protrudes around the rim of the basin. Keep the hair for your stock pot. Allow the eggs to solidify before removing the basin. Don the cassock, light the incense and chant monotonously for two hours. Do not make a habit of this.

UN OEUF IS UN OEUF

2 dozen eggs
4 oz butter
1 pt milk

Remove the eggs from your grandmother's mouth and separate them, placing one in the airing-cupboard, one on the roof and one round at Mrs Figgis's at No.6. Leave them there for a bit. Next, fetch them and whisk with the milk to a light froth. Melt the butter in a large saucepan and add the mixture. Stir continuously until it starts to thicken. Serve immediately onto warmed plates and start to eat. Go on eating. Eat until you can eat no more. Not another spoonful. Not a sausage. Not even a wafer-thin mint. Eat until you are as full as a badger. Eat until your belly is as taut as a drum. Now move gingerly to the sofa and lie very still. Abandon all thoughts of supper.

SCRAMBLED EGGS

2 eggs
2 cravats
2 deckchairs
1 Bakelite valve wireless
1 field telephone
1 air-raid siren
1 Supermarine Spitfire fighter 'plane
1 Hawker Hurricane fighter 'plane

Erect the deckchairs in the corner of a field somewhere in England. Now place an egg casually in each chair, draping a cravat around each in an unstudied yet elegant way. Turn on the wireless and tune it to a station playing the music of Glenn Miller or some such dance-band. Leave them to sit undisturbed for a while, ensuring that there is an adequate supply of reading material. During this period make sure that the engines of the 'planes are thoroughly warmed, but do not allow them to boil. Suddenly, without warning, sound the siren and ring the telephone frantically. You will find that the eggs will immediately run towards the aircraft. Allow them to take off as quickly as possible, after which they will be ready to serve.

Serves a few.

 13

UNDERWATER EGG

1 mini submarine
2 tin fish
6 fl oz German white wine
6 eggs
3 tbspn olive oil
3 tspn soy sauce
1 white iris
1 oz tar
salt
6 cockle shells

Take the submarine from its pen and submerge it in a pan of boiling water with the fish. Add hock. Now drop the eggs (still in their shells) in a pattern around it. After a short while they should start to explode, forcing the submarine towards the surface. Turn off the stove, shut all doors and windows and, in complete silence, listen for any signs of movement. Now, at a very low heat, slowly bring the eggs to periscope depth. Mix the oil and soy sauce together and drizzle it over the pan so that the fragments of egg float amidst a dark and ominous slick. Add tar and salt to taste. Drop in the flag so that it flutters on the surface. Using a slotted spoon, recover any of the debris which appears to be worth saving and serve on the cockle shells

*Most of these ingredients may be found
at Asdic superstores.*

POACHED EGGS

1 torch
1 balaclava
1 greatcoat
2 baskets

At the dead of night, preferably when there is no moon, don the balaclava and greatcoat, pick up the torch and the two baskets and, moving with great stealth, break into a nearby hen house, having first ascertained that it does not contain a host of aggressive and non-ovulating cockerels. Now edge ever closer until you can see the whites of their eggs and then steal as many of them as you possibly can, making sure that you do not put all of them into one basket. Run away silently for four minutes, setting your stride to medium. Try to get home without being seen. Boil the eggs.

Dixon's Patent Multifarious Egg-timer is recommended.

VOMIT AU VENTS (SIC)

12 vol-au-vent cases
a severe alimentary problem
butter

Vomit into the vol-au-vent cases. Glaze with the butter. Dispose of everything quietly.

BUFFALO-LEG DIPS

1 buffalo (or bison)
1 lb ground coriander seeds
1lb turmeric
1lb ground cumin seeds
4 gals olive oil

Wash your hands in a wash-basin and then wash the bison by hand. In a large frying-pan or portable swimming-pool, fry the spices in the oil for about ten minutes then set the mixture aside to cool. Remove the legs (the buffalo will rarely charge for this: if it does this may place you on the horns of a dilemma) and fry until they are a golden brown. Add the spice paste and cook for a further 36 hours, turning the legs from time to time. When done, allow to cool. Place several buckets of your favourite dips around the room, spread the legs on the carpet and serve as pre-supper nibbles. Keep the carcasses for stock.

FARMHOUSE PATÉ

1 small agricultural dwelling
3 tons butter
64 cwt pepper
36 cwt salt

Demolish the house, using explosive if necessary, and break the rubble into small cubes. Season and fry these in the butter until lightly browned. Now, a little at a time, liquidise until you have a cement-like paste. Place in a bowl and refrigerate.

Serve with a re-possession order.

 16

BABY KEBABS

6 12-lb babies
·1 red pepper
1 green pepper
1 yellow pepper
1 blue pepper
6 mashed bananas
2 oz napalm

Chop the peppers into one-inch pieces. Wipe each baby and put it on a skewer with the pieces of pepper. Put under a hot grill until everything starts to become crisp. Serve on a waterproof sheet, wrapped in a napkin with the mashed bananas and napalm.

THRUSH BEAKS ON TOAST

12 thrush beaks
1 loaf
anchovy sauce
butter or glue

Slice the bread and toast on one side. When done, place the bread toasted side down and spread with the butter or glue. Sprinkle the beaks evenly over this, ensuring they are in the correct pecking order and then cover them with a liberal coating of anchovy sauce. Toast until the beaks begin to open. Discard those that do not.

You may find pre-packed beaks in the supermarkets but, for the best flavour, scour your local pet-shops for some fresh ones going cheep.

II.   FLOATERS

PRAWNS IN GLASSES

1 lb peeled prawns
1 pr spectacles

Put the glasses on the prawns and look at them for a bit. Blink if you wish.

BOILED FLAT FISH

1 fish (pike is best)
10 cloves garlic
3 leeks
1 garden roller
1 pt water

Weigh the fish on your kitchen scales. Now, with a flat knife, remove the scales from the fish and place it upside down on a large even area of your patio, surrounding it with the garlic cloves and leeks. Next, push the roller over the ingredients until everything is about half an inch thick. Taking a spatula, prise the flat fish from the patio and chop into four inch squares. Add the water and cook in an electric toaster.

 20

KIPPER SURPRISE

2 kippers
1 Jiffy bag
1 stamp

Write your own address on the bag and place the kippers inside it. Seal the bag, stick the stamp on it (the post office can do this for you if you are squeamish) and place in the post box. Immediately take that long-awaited break in the Dordogne (this is best done at the height of summer) for at least three weeks. On your return home the parcelled kippers should be ready for you on your doormat. Open the bag and... voilà.

EEL DE FRANCE

6 french sticks
6 eels (gutted)
butter
salt and pepper

With a sharp knife slice open the bread. Butter them and set to one side. Take the eels and blanche them in a tramp-steamer for half an hour. Now place a whole eel in each bread stick. Trim off any overhanging eel and season to taste. Slips down a treat.

CURED HADDOCK

1 feverish haddock
24 paracetamol tablets
4 blankets

Put the haddock to bed immediately, covering it with the blankets and putting up with no nonsense whatsoever. Administer plenty of water and two paracetomol every four hours whilst allowing no visitors. After two days the fish will be at the correct temperature and you will be able to cook and eat it as normal, but remember to only allow it out if it is well wrapped up.

BATTERED COD

4 large cod
salt and pepper
1 eight-pound sledgehammer

Make sure that the fish is fresh by checking that the eyes are not cloudy. Too many fish these days are full of chemicals and additives so, if there is a choice, avoid using fish from an angler who has cortisone. Arrange the cod carefully on a large butcher's block, taking care not to damage the delicate fins, and season lightly. Now take the sledgehammer and beat the hell out of the fish until you feel better. Mind the bones.

WHALE MEAT À GEIGNE

1 blue whale
12 good eggs
16 Dover sole
8 oz old beans
3 lbs 'allo Vera
6 oz damesons
12 oz mulberries
16 hand-grenade safety-pins

Once you have bought it, clean and fillet the whale and bale out the stomach with a bucket. Now roast it on a Spit over the fire. Scramble the eggs, take off the heat and keep warm over a Hurricane lamp. Add the fruit, level out the mixture just below your ceiling and set aside out of the sun for a finest hour. Stuff the sole with the vegetables and then grill fiercely, if necessary depriving it of sleep for several days and hanging it upside down until it spills the beans. Now stuff the whale with the egg and fruit mixture and pin the sole to the underneath. Serve on a cocktail stick to a select few.

GREY MULLET WITH MUSTARD

1 1970s footballer
1 lb hot English mustard
1 Cliff Richard CD
6 oz plain flour
8 oz cheese footballs
oil

Remove the head from the footballer and throw the rest onto the cruel scrap heap of sporting history. Rub the mustard into the hair and leave the head on a spike by a fence. Now put the CD on your player, turn the volume to zero and listen to it, through headphones, for fifteen minutes. Next drop the head into the flour, dribble the oil onto it and kick it into the dining-room. Add the cheese footballs and immediately fall over and accuse one of your guests of tripping you up. Make sure he or she is sent to the scullery.

A SURFEIT OF LAMPREYS

21 lampreys
fish oil
salt and pepper

String and season the lampreys and fry until lightly browned in the oil. Eat twenty of them.

24

ASSISTED PLAICE

1 plaice
8 six-inch nails
4 gills water
2 oz thyme
8 whales

Help the plaice off with its skin and lead it to the grill pan. Make it comfortable on a bed of nails and sprinkle some water over it. Turn the grill to medium and, if you have one, close the door to ensure that the fish does not lie in a draught. Give it a little thyme. Meanwhile put the whales into a large pot. After about ten minutes, take the plaice to the school of whales. It should not be Eton at this stage. Allow the fish to mature, regularly testing its pupils to see what has been absorbed. When you are happy with the results, take it out of the water and leave it in bewilderment and confusion. After a year off, possibly travelling overseas, keep it at one degree for three years.

Makes four helpings.

FISH & CHIPS WITH SOUTHERN COMFORT

1 deep armchair
4 cushions
1 foot-stool
1 blanket

Take the ingredients to the English Channel coast. Buy a cod lot from a nearby takeaway. Place the chair facing out to sea. Plump up the cushions, position the stool, sit down and eat at leisure. Keep the blanket to hand in case the breeze picks up.

DEAR JOHN DORY

1 medium-sized John Dory
(as a guideline, Doris Stokes was under 6' 3")
1 sheet writing-paper
1 envelope
1 pen

This is not as expensive as it sounds. Keep the fish in the fridge for as long as it interests you. When this is no longer the case, take the pen and the paper and write down words to the effect that, whilst it was great fun to have it nestling amongst the milk cartons, bacon, sausages and white wine for a while, the fish no longer has that sparkling look in its eye, you no longer feel shivers down your dorsal area and, frankly, personal hygiene has become something of a problem. You feel a sense of *fin de siècle* and that the time has come to scale down your relationship, move on and perhaps introduce other foodstuffs into the fridge. If nothing else, the fridge needs its space. It is perhaps unnecessary to mention the fact that you have caught the eye of a basking shark. Put the letter in the envelope and leave it next to the fish. Expect it to have left by the weekend.

II. FLOATERS

III. FEATHERS

COQ AU VAN

1 chicken
1 roll of self-adhesive draught-excluder
1 small van

Open the rear doors of the van and apply the draught excluder carefully around the opening so as to ensure that the doors will be airtight. Place the chicken on greaseproof paper inside the van and close the doors. Drive around for a while (twenty minutes per pound-weight of chicken) at 27 m.p.h., increasing to 42 m.p.h. for the last twenty minutes. Having established that the chicken is thoroughly dead, carry on driving, ensuring that you stick to the relevant speed limits, until you arrive at a friend's house. Get them to cook it for you.

BOMB-BAY DUCK

1 10,000-lb duck
500 lbs explosive
salt and pepper
800 oranges
1 Avro Lancaster Mk. V
1 large cumulo nimbus cloud

Remove the ears from the duck and stick them to the wall. Now be careful what you say. Hang the explosive for a few days until it is high. Pluck the duck (be warned: the feathers can get everywhere, so you may get down on your hands and knees), stuff with the explosive, season and surround it with the oranges.
Load this into the bomber, start all four engines and taxi to the end of the runway. When cleared by the control tower, take off, immerse everything in the cloud, peel your eyes and head on a bearing of 135°. Avoiding flak batteries and searchlights whenever possible, jettison the whole lot over a vital industrial target. Head for home.

A ROMANTIC DUCK

1 duck
1 freshly-cut red rose
2 candles
1 box Belgian chocolates
100 ml eau de parfum
6 oz ribbon noodles
1 self-penned poem

Place the duck in the centre of the table, put the rose in its beak and flank it on both sides with the candles. Gently lay the chocolates and perfume in front of it, having first ensured that they are gift-wrapped with plenty of ribbon noodles. Light the candles, sit down quietly next to the duck and, in a small but portentous whisper, recite the poem. This recipe works equally well with diving sea-birds, so you could forget the Duck and have a Shag (or Pullet, if you must) instead. In this instance you can leave out the poem.

You can also repeat this process for a lark.

TAWNY OWL

4 small owls
1 oz sage
2 cups tawny port
2 stems raw horseradish

Take your fishing rod to a fast-running stream at dusk and catch four small owls. Clean them but do not pluck them as their plumage is a major part of their charm. Rotate the head of each bird seven times and then marinade them wisely for two hours in the port and sage. After this, wrap them individually in cooking-foil parcels, making sure to fold the seams neatly and place on a baking tray in the oven at number twooo. When there is no longer any discernible hooting, unwrap the parcels and serve on skewers with the raw horseradish.

PARROT CAKE

1 perch (filleted)
1 large parrot
6 oz Polyfilla
3 oz polyunsaturated spread
4 After Eight mints (chopped)

Grill the perch until lightly browned and set to one side. Put the parrot at its ease by finally revealing to it the identity of a pretty boy and then get it to put the kettle on. Once it has learnt to do this it may do so over and over again. When boiled, pour the water over the filler and mix until you have a paste. Allow to cool. Taking a small hammer, hit the parrot crisply over the head (you will find that parrots stun easily) and remove the breast. Fashion the parrot into noisettes and stuff with the paste. Put them in a baking tray, cover with the spread and cook for twenty minutes. When ready, place the parrot on the perch, garnish with the pieces of After Eight and serve repeatedly.

ROAST PTARMIGAN

1 large ptarmigan
1 diphthong (separated and finely grated)
4 fl oz cuckoo spit
3 oz late-night capers
oil

Place the bird on the kitchen table, pull up a chair, sit down and watch it for six hours. If there is no sign of movement, pronounce the ptarmigan dead, spitting out the 'p' and the 't' in one movement. Pluck it, clean it, stuff it with its own feathers and roll it in the diphthong and a little of the spit (you can collect some of yours from the kitchen walls to add to the cuckoo's if you wish). Brown in the oil and then cook slowly in an electric kettle. Wing and garnish with the capers.

CUSTERED

1 grouse
2 fl oz cochineal
1 bow and arrows
6 Wagon Wheels

Mount the grouse on a pot stand in the centre of the kitchen (if you are using a lot of these, make sure you keep your last one for this recipe). With a milk brush, paint the cochineal onto your cheeks and forehead, pluck a few quills from the bird and fix them to your head with a large elastic band. Now circle the grouse menacingly, letting out the occasional blood-curdling shriek or yelp. After three minutes, unleash the entire contents of your quiver at the bird until it resembles a feathery pin-cushion. Finally, remove the top of its head with a sharp knife. Garnish with the chocolates. Go out for a beer with the chaps.

CHRISTMAS FEAST

12 chicken drumsticks
10 M.C.C. membership cards
9 oz ladies fingers
8 pts milk
7 Swan Vestas matches
6 geese
5 fl oz Gold Blend coffee
3 oz French mustard
2 fl oz Dove shampoo
1 partridge

Put the chicken, geese and partridge into a roasting-pan. Cut the mustard into small pieces and coat the birds. Flash in the pan and then leave in a festive oven for two hours. For the last half-hour surround them with the okra. Meanwhile put the milk, coffee and shampoo into a blender and whisk to a froth. When the birds are cooked, take them out of the oven and scatter broken matches all over them. Fill eleven piping bags with the mixture and decorate the roasted meat. Garnish with the cards. Ring up four girlfriends and invite them to dinner.

TRICORN HAT

3 cobs corn
1 pheasant
1 pt beef stock
1 pt fish stock
2 lbs tomatoes (allowed to rot)
1 lb stale bread
2 pts water

Mix the two stocks together. Now form a triangle with the cobs and place them on the head of the pheasant. Next place the pheasant in the stocks and leave outside in all weathers, from time to time hurling the rotten tomatoes at it. Add bread and water. After three days, having removed it from the stocks, hang the bird at the far end of your kitchen. Sit down with pencil and paper, draw a picture of it and then cut it into four pieces. Expect no further trouble.

This would go well with a small side-dish like
chalk and cheese.

GROUSE AND CARP

1 grouse
1 carp
2 teeth (gritted)

Imprison the grouse until it starts to moan. If it stamps its feet, pay no attention. Meanwhile place the fish on a chopping-board and remove the scales with a flat knife. It may not take this lying down but ignore it if it expresses dissatisfaction with your technique. Cry its eyes out but remember that these should be sparkling and bright. Complain bitterly to your fishmonger if this is not the case. Now position the bird and the fish on the grill pan, sigh deeply, and toast morosely. Next, shed tears copiously over the dish and garnish with gnashings of teeth. Add a fuss which you have made earlier. Tear out your hair, wring your hands, beat your breast and serve reluctantly.

Have a good whine with this.

QUAIL

8 oz liver
1 lily
1 quail
4 fl oz cold sweat
1 white feather
3 fl oz whisky
2 oz grit
4 oz poltroon

Liquidise the liver and the lily and set aside. Drag the quail from behind the sofa, pluck and stand it in iced water until it gets cold feet. Now remove its heart, stuff with the lily liver paste and drizzle the sweat over it in a rain of terror. Stand outside to get the wind up. Next drop it into boiling water and blanche until it turns pale and the flesh starts to creep. Add the feather and the Dutch courage, sprinkle with grit and serve with the poltroon.

You could make a hare stand on end
or try this with chicken.

IV. FLESH

BEEF WELLINGTON

1 rib of beef
1 gumboot
1 pt toilet water
1 cup Napoleon brandy
8 oz Prussian prunes

Place the meat in the boot with the brandy (introduce the Napoleon into the Wellington slowly, otherwise it may react) and the Water from the Loo. Season to taste. Microwave at exactly 6.15 p.m. for quite a long time. Add the prunes at the last minute.

If you are short of time, try Lamb Wellington:
book a long weekend alone in a remote farmhouse in North Wales. Shake the lamb's tail twice and have the time of your life. If possible, it is better if the lamb is locally reared.

JAMAICAN HOT POT

1 oz Jamaican grass cuttings (jointed)
1 pkt cigarette papers
1 box matches

Just roll up, light up and puff away. Nothing else will matter. If you have guests in the dining-room waiting for dinner, who cares? Afterwards, using both hands, eat everything described in this book.

EARL STEW

1 earl
12 ant livers
61 pts water
1 bay leaf
1 oz chives
1 cwt conkers
salt and pepper
1 tspn brown sugar
1 dozen rabbit ears

Dust off the earl and remove his belt and any inherited traits. In a large cauldron with brass fittings, bring the water to the boil and then drop in the earl (taking care not to damage his seat), folding in the arms and legs if necessary, and the ant livers. Add the bay leaf and plenty of salt and pepper. Turn the heat down, add the chives and conkers and simmer for six generations in the shade of a family tree. Just before serving, sprinkle with the sugar to remove any residual bitterness in the earl. Serve with a simple rabbit-ear salad. Remember to say your grace before starting.

BUTTERED SOLICITOR

1 solicitor
6 prs briefs
1 chamber-pot
4 oz butter
1 face-flannel
1 12-volt battery-charger
6 torch bulbs

Using a potato-peeler, remove all hair from the solicitor. Bend the solicitor until you can force the head into the other aperture, place it carefully in the chamber-pot and surround with the briefs. Add all the butter and cover with the flannel. Now connect the charger so that the red terminal is attached to the head and the black one to the genitals. Charge overnight.
In the morning disconnect the charger. Remember to use rubber gloves as the dish will be at full voltage. Allow the solicitor to discharge a little into a small bowl and then garnish the dish by pushing the bulbs into small incisions in the skin. Convey to the table and serve at or around dusk without prejudice. Ask your guests to read prepared statements about the quality of the meal.

GINGER TOM YUM

1 domestic cat (male)
6 cloves garlic
2 onions
1 small tortoise
2 oz ginger
6 oz Cheshire cheese (grated)
6 ft string
Tabbyasco sauce*

Starting from scratch and summoning up all your curiosity, kill the cat nine times and skin it (there are many ways to do this). Remove the feet with a claw-hammer. Chop the onions and garlic. Remove the tortoise shell (you may already have one left over from Jugged Hair, see p68), add to the ginger and grind to a powder. Mix all this together with a cat's whisk, stuff the animal and roast in an excessive oven for an hour. When ready, put a plate on the kitchen floor and, reaching up as high as you can, drop the cat so that it lands the right way up on it. Cover with the cheese, add a dash of hot sauce and serve on a cradle of string. Yum yum!

* Dixon's Patent Tabbyasco Sauce is recommended.

SQUIRREL FLAMBÉ

1 squirrel (warning: may contain nuts)
6 fl oz lighter fuel

Remove the harmonica from the squirrel's paws. Now dip the long fluffy tail into the lighter fuel. Light and retire immediately, not forgetting to inform your employer of your decision.

MOBSTER THERMIDOR

1 violent gangster
1 horse's head
2 oz butter
2 tbspn plain flour
1 pt milk
1 lb mushrooms
1 tspn mustard seed
1 pt cream
1 sq ft Mafia ratting

Don an apron, remove the flesh from the mobster and chop it into bite-sized pieces, setting aside any hidden firearms. Now melt the butter in a violin case and stir in the horse's head and the flour over a medium heat for 1 minute. Add the milk and mushrooms and cook until the mixture boils and thickens. Stir in the mustard seed and mobster flesh. Add the cream and serve on the ratting.

VOLE VENTS

4 voles
salt and pepper

Season the voles and place under a hot grill for ten minutes. Now, using a vole-wrench, place them on a plate and then blow on them until they are cool enough to eat.

You could follow these with Mole Teasers, (p59).

HAMBURGERS

1 butterfly net
3 actors
5 Hamlet cigars (grated)
hair oil

Go to your local theatre and wait by the stage door until the interval. Using the butterfly net, catch three actors and smuggle them home. Remove their make-up with a potato-peeler, discard their costumes, break their legs and place them in a food processor, feet uppermost. They may take an age to die but, when finely minced (if they are not already), hold the mixture briefly in the palm of your hand, add the tobacco, form into cakes and cast them into the oil. Fry earnestly, turning once. When you have eaten the actors, be sure to tell them how good they were. It is bad luck to mention Big Macbeths (see p74).

NOUVELLE BURGERS

2 oz minced beef
6 small radishes
vegetable oil

Separate the mince into individual granules of meat and fry them in the oil one at a time until they start to brown but remain rare in the middle. Using large white plates (minimum 12-inch diameter), put two of these onto each plate and serve with a radish.

RUSSIAN DOGS DINNER

1 cat
1 chihuahua
1 King Charles spaniel
1 standard poodle
1 Rottweiler
1 dog lead
salt and pepper

Clean and skin the animals. Cover with salt and pepper until they are in season. Now, starting with the smallest, place it inside the next largest. When the Rottweiler is stuffed tie it together tightly with the lead and roast in a medium oven for eight hours and then let it sit and wait. Go for a walk. When the juices run clear, whistle and they should come back immediately. If you are still uncertain as to whether everything is cooked, throw a stick. If nothing moves, it is ready. Keep the bones for your dog.

LEGO LAMB

6 lamb chops
12 4x2 Lego blocks
6 2x1 Lego blocks
salt and pepper

Finely grate the large blocks and set aside in a bowl. Make small incisions into the meat. Push the small blocks into these cuts and season well. Now sprinkle the grated Lego over the chops and grill under a medium heat until all the plastic has melted. Leave to harden and then serve to people who have false teeth. On no account use this to build a small scale-model of a bungalow after cooking.

CLARIFIED BUTTER

1 goat
1 Encyclopaedia Britannica
1 Brewer's Dictionary of Phrase and Fable
1 table of logarithms
1 collected works of Shakespeare
1 anthology of the works of Nietzsche
1 collected letters of Proust
1 Oxford Companion to Literature
1 portfolio of drawings by Rolf Harris
1 Little Book of Calm
1 history of the Bay City Rollers
1 Wisden Cricketers' Almanac
1 knob of butter

Invite the goat into your sitting room and make sure that it is comfortable and relaxed, even if at the end of its tether. Possibly over a glass of hock, don your horn-rimmed spectacles, stroke your beard and in a sympathetic but firm manner ask the animal if there are any vexing questions of an existential or more practical nature that have been bothering it for some time. With skilful reference to your books, attempt to edge the creature closer to the Meaning of Life. Once you feel that it has begun to see the light, fold in the knob and turn it into cheese.

WALNUT WHIP

10 oz walnuts
2 oz chestnuts
8 fl oz good hock
1 saddle beef
2 Palomino peppers
2 sticks horseradish
2 oz Epsom salt
1 riding crop (freshly harvested)
1 Spurs football programme
oil and vinegar dressage
2 armfuls of hay
1 go-kart

P lace all the ingredients in a long line on your work-surface, ensuring that you don't put the go-kart before the horseradish. Fill a stirrup cup with the nuts and put them in hock. Leave to marinade for an hour. Grind the peppers and horseradish to a powder and rub into the beef. Season with the Epsom salt. Now grate the crop over the top and place on a roasting-dish in the oven for two hours. It is important that the temperature is stable. While this is cooking, cut the programme into one-inch strips and, when there is half an hour of cooking time left, lay these over the the beef. Once ready, place the whole dish on the seat of the go-kart, garnish with the hay and drive it to the table.

NUT ROAST

8 tin soldiers
salt and pepper
8 oz chipped potatoes

I t is best to read and understand this recipe before you start cooking. Pre-heat the cooker to 200° Fahrenheit, head for the oven, and then kneel down in front of it, remove any accoutrements such as hats, jewellery, spectacles, wigs, etc., and place your head on the middle shelf, ensuring that the heat will circulate easily. Stay in this position for two hours, whilst remembering to turn your head over halfway through and baste regularly. If you can't stand the heat, get out of the kitchen. Once you feel you are ready, return to an upright position and allow yourself to stand for ten minutes in the scullery. Now place the chips on your shoulders. Next, depending on your usual preference, remove the top of your head with either a knife or an egg-spoon. Season to taste, sit down at the table and, using the spoon and dipping the soldiers, slowly devour your brain. If you are in company, you may find that conversation tails off a little towards the end. Do not attempt to play football or to drive after you have finished eating.

TOAD-IN-THE-HOLE

1 medium-size male toad
6 oz mushrooms
2 lbs earth
salt and pepper

Put the toad into an airtight tin and wait until it croaks. Now fill a large casserole dish with the earth then, with a tablespoon, dig a small hole in the centre of it. Take the toad and carefully remove its penis with the minimum of fuss, drop the toad into the hole, add the mushrooms and season to taste. Now fill up the hole with the scooped-out earth, cover and bake in a medium oven for two hours. While this is happening gently sauté the severed appendage in a little butter. When the dish is cooked, serve immediately and garnish with the toad's tool.

Croak Monsieur makes a good accompaniment to this.

IV. FLESH

V. FLANKS

TARKA DHAL

1 otter
1 hand-mirror
20 birch twigs
7 oz lentils
1 onion
8 cloves garlic
2 tspn cumin seeds
8 oz dust

First, peel the otter. Now reprimand it severely for some real or imagined transgression and leave it to reflect in front of the mirror. Build a small dam across the corner of the kitchen with the birch twigs, lentils and cumin seed. Fill the dam with boiling water from the kettle to within an inch of the top of the dam. Now drop the otter into the water, add the onion and garlic cloves and leave it to gently stew until the spring, topping up the water level from time to time when necessary. When the first daffodils appear, cut a handful and spread them on a platter and place the now ready otter on top. Sprinkle with dust and carve at the table.

ALMOND AND CABBAGE PARCELS

4 oz slivered almonds
1 cabbage
1 sq yd brown paper

Wrap the cabbage and almonds in the brown paper and post them to a friend or your local M.P. Go on holiday for two weeks.

PAPERBACK RAITA

1 trashy novel (you can find these in all bad bookshops)
1 pt yoghurt
1 cucumber
1 tspn cumin seeds

Beat the yoghurt in a bowl until smooth and creamy. Add all the other ingredients and mix. Refrigerate until just before eating. Note that reading the novel may make you vomit.

GREEK MUSHROOMS

1 lb mushrooms
6 oz gorgon zola cheese
tartarus sauce

Keep the mushrooms in Stygian gloom until they are thoroughly demoralised. They are quite used to this, as they tend to exist under something of a cloud which does not sit well with the rising sun. Heat them gently in a Pan, stirring continuously to ensure that nothing Styx to the bottom. Now, looking into a hand-mirror and not directly at the food, add the cheese to the mix until it has melted. Spoon over a little of the sauce and serve uncomprehendingly.

ROSE HIP SYRUP

1 dating-agency telephone number
12 oz honey
12 oz treacle

Contact the agency and search their records until you find a woman called Rose. Arrange to meet her, remove one of her legs and lop off the top joint. Put it into a blender with the honey and treacle and mix until you have a syrup. What you do with it now is entirely up to you. Offer to give your new companion a lift home. It's the least you can do.

STUFFED TOMATOES

6 large tomatoes
2 small throw-cushions

Slice open the cushions and extract the stuffing. Place it in a mixing bowl. With a sharp knife, cut the top inch off each tomato and remove the insides. Now fill each tomato with the stuffing and replace the 'lids'. Take them to the dining-room and place one on each chair. Cover with material that matches the seats.

STUFFED EARWIGS

300 earwigs
1/100th oz sausage meat
3/100th oz bread crumbs
1/100th oz sage and onion mix
1 ft ground skirting-board

Taking each earwig in turn, remove the head, pincers and outer shell and discard. Next put each one into its own dustbin of water. It is important that they are kept separate at this stage because they can be worryingly territorial, even after death. While they are soaking for two hours, mix the bread crumbs and stuffing mix with water until you have a porridge, Now take each earwig and stuff it with the mixture. Place on a baking tray, scatter the grated wood around it and roast for twenty minutes. When ready serve under a large rock.

ONIONS ELLA

2 strings onions (about 16 onions per string)
1 8-oz frog (cleaned)
1 small beret
1 bicycle
2 prs bicycle-clips
1 fencing foil
oil

Take the bicycle and drizzle the oil onto the gears, sprockets and all other moving parts. Drape one string of onions over each side of the handle-bars. Now take the frog and place the bicycle-clips securely around its ankles and position the beret at a rakish angle on the top of its head (should you have one left over in the fridge, you could at this point add a stripy jumper, but this should be removed twenty minutes before the cooking time is up to avoid curdling). Secure this with a small meat skewer. When attired to your satisfaction, place the frog on the saddle of the bicycle. Do not worry if its back legs do not reach the pedals because frogs, and in fact most amphibians, never forget how to ride a bicycle. Cover with the foil and cook in a preheated oven at No.6 for an hour. After the hour is up, go round to No.6 again and bring it back home to eat.

58

MOLE TEASERS

6 moles from your lawn
fresh chopped parsley or coriander
1 dodo egg*
flour
salt and pepper
giraffe dripping*

Taunt the moles by saying something like 'Hey Moley, look at this very interesting object' or 'What's your favourite colour?'. Now bury them in the garden. After a while, exhume them, bone and chop very finely. Grill the dodo egg until it is rare, put into a bowl and add the parsley or coriander. Mix well, until you have a smooth paste. Now roll the mixture into little balls about half an inch in diameter and coat with the flour and seasoning. Fry until dark brown. Serve as a tempting appetiser but, just as your guests are about to eat them, whisk them away and back to the kitchen.

* Dixon's patented requisites are recommended here.

FRENCH LEAVES

1 borrowed novel
6 rocket leaves
2 curry leaves
1 bay leaf
2 oz gold leaf
6 oz long hops

Take a leaf out of someone else's book. Now mix all the ingredients together, whilst, with unwavering concentration, leaving the long hops. Go on holiday without telling anybody.

GRILLED STICK INSECT

130 medium-sized stick insects
1 jar Marmite

Remove the legs from the insects with a pair of vole-tweezers and discard. Do not waste time trying to remove the wings as they don't have any. Now dip the insects into the Marmite and place them under a hot grill for two minutes. Allow to cool and place in a jug. When seated, shake the jug and throw the contents onto the table-cloth. Allow each guest in turn to attempt to pick up one stick insect without disturbing any of the others. If successful, the guest may eat it and try again. If other stick insects are disturbed, however, the guest must stop eating and the turn passes to the left. Given the fact that they are covered in a glutenous yeast extract, this should give you a good hour's rest before trudging back to the kitchen to resume your forced labour.

GLAZED CARROTS WITH WAFFLES

8 carrots
1 sock
parsley

Place the carrots in a line on your worktops. Now pull up a stool, sit down in front of them and regale the vegetables with a series of tedious anecdotes about your school-days, grass-cutting adventures, DIY mishaps, golf matches, favourite shaving soaps, bidding errors whilst playing bridge, your new car, Association Football, etc. After a while (probably sooner than you might think) the carrots will glaze over. Now place them in a bowl and put a sock in it. Serve with a sprig of parsley.

VI.   ODDITIES

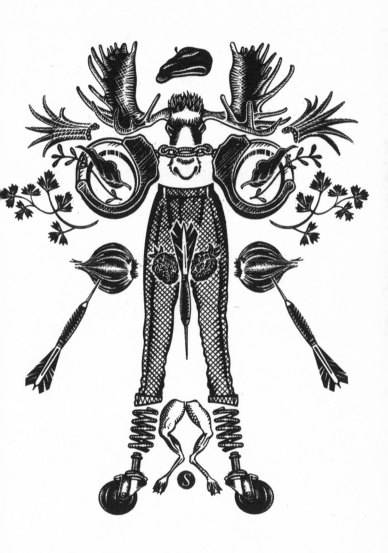

TROUSER RISOTTO

1 mole
8 oz long-grain rice
2 apples
6 flies
olive oil
salt and pepper
1 pr trousers

Skin the mole and discard the carcass. Cook the rice as usual and add the flies. Place an apple in each pocket, rub the oil and seasoning into the seat of the trousers, inside and out, put them on and run around until they are at 103.4° Fahrenheit. Allow to cool by sitting in the fridge for ten minutes. Press flat, add the mole skin and serve on the rice.

Dixon's Patent Kitchen Trouser-press is recommended.

CHICKEN MOOSE

1 Canadian moose
1 shotgun
1 telephone

Stand the moose in the centre of the kitchen, ensuring that you have left the door to the back garden open. Now aim the gun at the animal and threaten to blow it away in a totally uncompromising manner. If necessary, sneer menacingly, show it the numerous mounted heads surrounding your fireplace, some of which date back to the days of your great-grandfather, and let a cartridge or two off into the ceiling. Do this until the moose runs away in terror. Ring up your local Chinese or Indian restaurant and order a take-away. Go and get it.

OLD MRS FIGGIS'S SPRING PIE

4 three-inch coil springs (leaf springs tend to wilt)
1 tspn oil (not GTX)
1 tbspn castor sugar
2 castors (swivel-mounted are easier to peel)
1 litre custard
1 onion
2 raspberries
1 jailbait (young whitebait)

Marinade the springs and castors in the oil for seven months. While this is going on, peel the onion, keeping the skin and discarding the rest. Chop the onion skin into two-inch dodecahedrons and dust them with a duster and then sugar. Fry them briefly at 27,000 feet and allow to cool on the back of a camel. When the marinade is ready, throw the onion skins into it from a distance of at least twelve yards. Gut the jailbait, fillet it and thrust it head-first into the mixture, holding it there until the wriggling stops. Cover with custard and serve with brown bread or cake. When you have finished eating, suck the raspberries to take away the taste.

GRILLED BASS

1 double-bass
4 oz powdered French horn
6 small wholemeal drum rolls
6 small tympani (skinned)
4 drops Gentian viola
1 tuba tomato purée

Pluck the double-bass and separate it into two single pieces, ensuring that one half has the 'G' and 'D' strings, the other the 'A' and 'E' strings and removing the sounding-post. Do not use the bridge as this would be going too far. Dust with the powdered horn, cover with tomato purée and place under a hot grill for the whole of the first movement of your favourite symphony. Try to ensure that you do not inhale any of the powder as this may make you cough during the quiet bits. Add the viola and serve in the small skinned tympani with the drum rolls.

BANGERS, MASH AND DUCK

2 lbs potatoes
1 pt milk
8 cloves garlic (crushed)
12 squibs
salt and pepper
1 lb rocket leaves

Peel and boil the potatoes and then mash them with the milk and garlic. Season to taste. Make a large mound of the mash on your plates and push several squibs into each one. Light the ends of the squibs at the table and watch your guests diving for cover. Serve with a rocket salad and eat with Fawkes. Redecorate your dining-room.

PAWN COCKTAIL

2 oz red lettuce
1 oz fresh, young, small dandelion leaves
1 chess set (not frozen)
12 oz french beans (cold, very fine and cooked al dente)
12 asparagus spears (freshly cooked, cold)
6 fl oz history
1 lemming*
seafood sauce
fennel (fresh fronds)

This is a recipe to live for! Remove all the Kings, Queens, Bishops, Knights and Rooks (or Castles) from the chess set and discard safely. Now steep the 16 pawns in history. With a sharp saw, cut the board into sixteen 2x2 squares and place them in the fridge for ten minutes. When this is done, arrange the lettuce and dandelion leaves in small mounds on the 'squares'. Divide the pawns, beans and asparagus elegantly upon the mounds. Coat with the seafood sauce, decorate with the fennel and add a squeeze of lemming.

* In the absence of fresh produce, Dixon's Patent Lemming Juice is recommended.

JUGGED HAIR

12 oz hair
8 oz streaky bacon
4 celery sticks
2 onions
4 cloves garlic
1 small head of fennel
2 Bouquet Garni
6 fl oz Brilliantine

First, catch your hair. With the speed control set to high, hold an electric whisk close to your head until it becomes inextricably entangled in your barnet, you feel you are about to become a Red Indian war-trophy and the motor grinds to a halt with smoke pouring from the casing and sparks sputter in your ears. Now take a sharp pair of scissors and cut the machinery free. With your fingers, pick the hair from the whisk and attach each strand to your washing-line with clothes-pegs. Hang for up to five days (for a true gamey flavour it is advisable not to have used any shampoo for at least a week). Chop the bacon and vegetables finely and fry lightly in the brilliantine. Put these, the hair and the herbs into a large casserole, cover and simmer for three hours. Serve this to your guests but eat a small tortoise yourself. See who finishes first. Wear a hat at dinner.

If you have just spent a small fortune on a new hairstyle and do not want to use your own hair, you could take a dustpan and brush to your local barber's shop or, failing that, try shaving a drunken dog.

68

SESAME ENTRÉE

6 oz sesame seeds
40 thieves
1 guinea-pig or similar cavy
1 black sheep
6 camel humps
1 armful hay
8 oz presto sauce
12 oz sultanas
1 wicker laundry-basket
14 oz long-grain sand
10 oz Turkish Delight

Dry-roast the sesame seeds in a very hot skillet until they start to open. Catch the thieves and invite them into a large cauldron with the guinea-pig, not forgetting that 'please' is the magic word. Butcher the sheep and add the humps, hay, presto, open sesame seeds and sultanas, seal the lid and simmer for a thousand and one nights. When ready, open the cauldron, if you can, and strain through the laundry-basket. Serve on boiled sand and garnish with the Turkish Delight.

STIR-FRIED PORRIDGE

20 frog's legs
drawing-pins
1 cork pinboard
6 ins old lagging
1 pr handcuffs
1 pt custard
1 bucket
oil
6 fl oz black Tia Maria

Stretch the legs and pin them to the board.
Next wrap them in the lagging and leave them
there for a reasonable time. Do nothing more until
the end of this sentence. Now, place them behind the grill
and, once inside, make sure that none of them escape
by handcuffing them to the bars of the oven shelves.
Once they have turned a pallid grey colour, remove them
and place to one side. Fill a large bowl with the custard,
release the legs and drop them in so that they lie in custardy
splendour. Blend to a thick paste-like consistency.
Slop out the bucket, cover the bottom with oil and stir-fry
until the mixture starts to bubble. Add the Tia Maria and
serve time after time.

WESTERN SPAGHETTI

8 oz spaghetti
1 crow
100 dollar bills
7 mussels
6 fl oz good hock or Pinot Gringo wine, with a smoky finish
1 dirty dozen bad eggs
2 ugli fruit
10 galls Colt 45
1 wild bunch parsley
2 oz Indian tea
1 oz che root (grated)
1 oz arrowroot (grated)
4 oz true grit
Palomino pepper sauce
horseradish sauce

Rinse the spaghetti pieces to remove the starch and then hang 'em high to dry. Bring a pan of water to the boil and drop in the spaghetti and the crow. Add a fistful of dollars and the magnificent mussels, dead or alive. After only a few minutes turn the heat to low and introduce the good wine, the bad eggs and the ugli fruit. Simmer enigmatically. Now, through narrowed eyes, add a few dollars more, the beer and the parsley and cook for a further ten minutes. Strain and serve, sprinkling the dish with the tea, grated roots and grit. Add the sauces to taste. Eat at sunset.

GAME PIE

pastry
1 set darts
1 thimble
6 sardines
1 pack cards (shuffled)
1 hop
4 fl oz scotch whisky
8 marbles
4 dice (diced)
6 fl oz gin
2 fl oz rum
12 oz back of gammon (finely chopped)
1 halfpenny
10 pins
fresh cribbage

Line a pie-dish with the pastry, making sure that it fits snugly by putting in a few darts if necessary. Snap them if too long. Now make sure you have found the thimble and force the sardines into it. Remove the hearts from the pack and set aside for stock, keeping the highest picture card for later. This can be messy so remove your shirt and just leave a singlet on. Mix the remainder of the cards with the hop, scotch, marbles and diced dice and taste to ensure that one flavour does not monopolise the others. In a separate bowl, mix the other two spirits together to make your gin rummy (this will take patience). Now stir all the ingredients together with a poker whilst adding the gammon, fill the pie, add a pastry lid and shove in the halfpenny. Bake until brown, serve on a bed of boiled cribbage and set before the king which you saved earlier. Ideal for keeping your family happy in the winter. You could finish with a round of craps (watch out for trumps).

This is especially good if preceded by Alphabet Soup (see p10).

PUMPKIN PUDDING

1 family
1 bicycle-pump

Assemble all your relatives in one room of the house. Whilst they are chatting together in an animated fashion, approach each of them in turn from behind, insert the pump and inflate them until the skin is smooth. Now place them all in a large net and drop them into boiling water to blanche. Serve on cocktail sticks.

BIG MACBETH

1 toad
3 witches
6 eggs
1 newt's eye
1 frog's toe
1 lizard's leg (boned)
863 cloves garlic (peeled and crushed)
1 wolf
1 moth (male)
8 oz bat wool
6 oz ladies' fingers
1 oz hemlock root (finely grated)
1 tspn tartar sauce
6 fl oz baboon's blood
4 lbs earthworms
8 oz cobwebs
2 oz ghoul ash

As witches tend to go off easily, it is best to obtain three, although you will use only one for this recipe. Place the toad under a cold stone and leave it there for a month. Meanwhile, to the sound of thunder, if possible, wipe one of the witches with a towel, place her in a bowl and mix in the eggs, choosing carefully which witch you wish to whisk. Throw in the towel. Now place the mixture into a large pot and heat it until it starts to boil and bubble. Next add the pieces of amphibian and reptile and the garlic whilst still stirring, stirring, stirring until you have a broth. Now for the tricky bit: fill your sink with water and stand the wolf in it. Having distracted the creature by pointing a finger at the moon, suddenly extract one of its teeth, in one movement, with a pair of pliers. There may be a struggle at this point and you could find yourself left with muddy water and a howling wolf. Throw the tooth into the pot with the okra and the toad and leave to simmer. The wolf will probably bugger off. Holding the moth tightly between forefinger and thumb, slice off its testicles with one swipe of a sharp knife into a mixing bowl. Allowing the insect to flutter off muttering high-pitched deprecations, immediately add the wool to the bowl and knit until you have a tangled mess. Just before serving, add the hemlock, sauce and blood to the main pot, simmer for a few seconds and then spread over a tangle of worms. Garnish with the cobwebs, moth balls and ash.

Drink a good Graves and a range of spirits.

Serve this with Devilled Kidneys and Mice Pudding (see p94) or I Scream.

PHRASE FONDUE

1 cat
1 crow
1 pigeon
1 pt cockles
1 mole's heart
linseed oil
6 fl oz absinthe
2 oz nauseam
1 fruit bat
1 bee
1 tin worms
6 doorbells
French bread

Put the cat in a bag, ensuring that escape is impossible. Set aside for later. Now kill both the birds simultaneously with a large stone. Warm the cockles and the heart in a saucepan and add the crow and some oil. Next slowly introduce the absinthe. This is the crucial part as absinthe makes the heart/crow fondue. Simmer for absolutely ages. Add nauseam. Meanwhile carry your bat to the sink, sand it down and rub in some linseed oil, avoiding the area between its shoulders. Leave it to soak in. Remove the legs from the bee and then trim off the thighs and shins. Open a can of worms and put them and the bee's knees into the pot. Now peel the bells and add them, with the bat, to the mixture. Last of all, let the cat out of the bag, put it amongst the pigeons and drop them into the pan. After a further five minutes, eat with French bread.

76

PRESSED RAT AND WARTHOG

1 rat
1 warthog
3 apples
wrapping-paper
1 dog leg
2 dog feet
1 peg-leg
1 woodworm
2 oz Deroga tree bark
3 fl oz fresh cream
1 pr red jodhpurs
1 striped tie
1 3-legged sack
192 lbs ginger
2 drumsticks
1 toad (battered)
sweet wine

Place the rat in a trouser-press and tighten it until all the juice has been collected. Ensure that the meat is in a blue condition. Now skin the warthog, stuff it with the rat and place in a roasting-dish. Peel and de-tune the apples, wrapping paper around each one, and then position them, with the dog legs and feet, around the edges of the dish. Next grate the peg-leg, woodworm and bark and sprinkle this over the meat. After rollin' and tumblin' the meat in a strange brew of cream and rat juice, lay the jodhpurs over the top and then secure them with the tie. Put the whole dish into the sack and roast moderately from four until late, amplifying the heat for the last twenty minutes and passing the time by dreaming of tales of brave Ulysses. Take it back to your work surface, feel free to add a spoonful of sweet wine, and garnish with the ginger, drumsticks and toad.

I have served this to many politicians and I'm so glad to say that this recipe brought me a badge of honour – those were the days!

DOGGEREL

1 mackerel
1 pooch
3 eggs
1 pt hooch
1 pea
2 tomatoes
6 sprouts
3 potatoes

Taking the dog
And the mackerel too
Cover with hooch
And make a good stew

Place in a strong
And reliable dish
So the dog will eventually
Taste like a fish

Now take the tomatoes
A potato or three
And boil them in water
With sprouts and the pea

But don't make the vegetables
Soggy. You see
Al dente (that's crunchy)
Is how they should be.

Strain them and drain them
And place in a pot
Which you put in the oven
To keep them all hot

VI. ODDITIES

Now check that your dog-fish
Is ready to eat
By using a skewer
Then turn off the heat

Now place all the food
On a plate and take wine
To the guests at your table
And sit down to dine

VII. ENDINGS

STRAWBERRY PAVLOV

12 oz strawberries
sugar
single cream

Having discarded any that show the slightest lack of enthusiasm, place the strawberries in the fridge. Every day, at a regular time (10.30 a.m. would do), take them out of the fridge and sprinkle sugar over them. Do this for about a week. The strawberries will learn when their daily 'sugaring' is due. From the eighth day onwards do not sugar them at all. You will soon notice a light tapping sound from within the fridge. This will be the strawberries wondering what has happened to their daily dose of sugar. When fully trained, eat the strawberries with lots of cream and, if you wish, a spoon.

CHARLIE AND THE CHOCOLATE FACTORY

2 oz cocaine
1 lb cooking chocolate

In a small heavy-bottomed pan, melt the chocolate and stir in the white powder. Pour into ice-trays and place in the freezer for half an hour. Press out the solidified cubes and place one in your mouth, allowing it slowly to dissolve against your gums. Now you can really start cooking.

GOOSEBERRY FOOL

4 gooseberries
2 oz castor sugar
1 black leather chair
1 250-watt spotlight

Taking each gooseberry in turn, place it in the chair under the spotlight, dim any other lights and then bombard it for exactly two minutes with the sugar and a series of impenetrable questions ranging from the arcane to the trivial. When you first do this you should confine your questions to the subject of gooseberries or the gooseberry-related. This process, however, must be repeated and on this second occasion the questions should be as wide ranging as possible. Placing the other three back in the fridge, serve the gooseberry with the fewest correct answers to your guests.

TOBLERONE SQUARES

1 large Toblerone chocolate bar

Take the chocolate bar and break it into its constituent triangular pieces. Using a sharp knife, trim the pieces until they are square-shaped. Place in a bowl and serve with coffee after dinner.

 83

SPROUT ICE-CREAM

1 lb sprouts
1 pt double cream
Worcestershire sauce

Put the cream in a small pan over a low heat and reduce it to tears. Pour into a bowl and add the sprouts. Cover with aluminium foil and place in the freezer, stirring occasionally to prevent crystals from forming. Serve with Worcestershire sauce. Your children will either learn to love sprouts or learn to hate ice-cream.

RICE PUDDING CRACKLING

1 rice pudding
salt

Make a rice pudding using, if you wish, a recipe. Leave it to cool and then carefully remove the skin from the top of the pudding. Throw away the rest of the pudding emotionally but bravely despite any misgivings. Remember it is for the greater good. Make deep cuts into the skin, rub in plenty of salt and place under a hot grill for ten minutes. Serve as canapés or as a side-dish to roasted chocolate.

PINEAPPLE UPSIDE-DOWN PUDDING

1 pineapple
2 oz sugar

Slice the top off the pineapple and hollow out the fruit. Put the contents, with a little water and the sugar, in a saucepan and bring to the boil. When it is a simmering pulp, pour it back into the hollow pineapple and cover with the 'lid'. Take this to the table immediately and, when standing next to a guest, turn it upside-down in one movement.

APPLE TURNOVER

8 apples
1 oz strong Cheddar cheese (cubed)

Place the apples on a plate with the stalks uppermost. With your fingers, remove all the stalks. Now, taking each apple in turn, pick them up, invert them and place them back on the plate. Serve with the Cheddar.

CRÈME BRÛLÉE

1 pt double cream
5 egg yolks
2 oz castor sugar
1 tbspn water
4 drops vanilla essence
1 blowtorch

Whisk the egg yolks, sugar, cream and vanilla. Place the mixture in ramekins and bake in a bain-marie for 40 minutes. Allow to cool. In a heavy saucepan, dissolve the sugar and water and cook until the sugar caramelises. Pour the topping into the ramekins. Now light the blowtorch so you have a roaring flame and blast the the topping until it starts to brown and your overhead kitchen cupboards have caught fire and are belching acrid black smoke which is already billowing up the stairs. A fortuitous gas leak from your ageing Flavell Equerry cooker will, by now, be accelerating the process. Within minutes the kitchen will have turned into a blazing inferno with the plastic sleeving from your sub-standard wiring falling in flaming lumps onto your tinder-dry pine dresser which, within seconds, will turn into a grim pastiche of a Shaker cremation. Your entire house is now under threat, immediately causing you to question the wisdom of choosing the deflated premiums as offered by the Chimera Insurance Company of PO Box 13, Goole, Yorkshire. By now you will have been forced into the front garden sporting just the cooking apron which you had chosen to wear as an alternative to the possibility of splashing cream onto your carefully-pressed dinner outfit, up which flames are currently licking in the main bedroom. The sound of the paper-thin party wall dividing the two delightful and irreplaceable 15th-century, semi-detached, thatched cottages, within which you and your 19-stone, psychopathic next-door-neighbour dwell, collapsing adds to the frisson of excitement which you are now feeling. At this point the aforementioned neighbour

 86

appears, towering over the two-foot garden fence, holding above his head the meat cleaver which, to your certain knowledge, he is in the habit of utilising to control the population of his menagerie of Malaysian pot-bellied pigs that he maintains in his spare bedroom. At this moment the usual discussion concerning the weather seems inappropriate. Your telephone, fortunately, is still within reach just inside the front door. It remains a moot point as to whether a phone call to the Police or the Fire Brigade is the most pressing option. Before this decision can be made, you hear beside you the sound of the fence splintering. You half turn and... you awake in a cold sweat on your bed to the sound of an old lady singing to a pig in her back yard. Your guests will be here in twenty minutes and you are nowhere near ready for them. A sense of panic grips you as you realise that the dinner party will be a disaster. Why do you bother to entertain like this. It's the same every time. It can't be worth it. Next time, eat out. The insurance cheque might just cover the cost

RAISINS TO BE CHEERFUL (PART 1)

12 oz raisins
pepper
6 oz Vim
2 pts Smiles bitter
2 jokers from a pack of cards
1 bucket water
1 bottle bubbly

This recipe is best for two people. Pepper up the raisins, cover them in the Vim and nibble them while you drink the beer. Now take the cards and play Snap with your companion. This could be very tense. After a while, take the bucket and a deep breath and wet yourself. Follow this up by drinking the Champagne. Keep doing this until you feel jolly good.

PANCAKE LANDING

2 lbs plain flour
2 dozen eggs
8 pts milk
3 pts oil
lemon juice
1 bag castor sugar

To make the batter, sift the flour into a bowl and then add the egg and the milk, stirring constantly. Heat the oil in a tin bath. Pour the batter into the bath and cook until the underside is a golden colour. Toss it in the air to cook the other side. Make a large quantity of these. Take them upstairs and carefully lay them out flat on the floor between your bedroom and bathroom doors. Ensure that all the carpet is covered and then sprinkle lemon juice and sugar lightly over them.

RUM BAABAA

1 pt dark rum
2 black sheep
1 bath sponge

Grease a baking-tin and cover the bottom and sides with the sponge. Sheer the sheep and chop into one-inch cubes. Ram the cubes into the tin and top up with the rum. Get your dog to steer the dish into the oven and cook at a low setting for an hour. Now divide into six portions and take one to the table. The others will follow. Any leftovers can be put into a Tupperware container and refrigerated.

CAMEMBERT DU PONT

1 Camembert
1 sock
1 hammer
1 masonry nail
1 pr waders

Take the Camembert and place it in the sock. Now, carry this to a nearby river (preferably tidal) with a bridge. Depending on the depth of the water, don the waders if necessary and set off for the central arch. Nail the sock to the underside of the bridge. Leave immediately. Spend some time in Khartoum.

 89

CHEESE & BILLIARDS

2 oz Brie (this must be very runny)
2 oz Roquefort
1 oz Parmesan
1 oz Edam
4 oz Stilton
3 oz hundreds and thousands
1 billiard table
1 blowtorch
2 sticks celery
2 pkts cheese and onion crisps

Shut the stilton away in a kitchen drawer. Now inform all the other pieces of cheese what you are about to do, but keep the stilton in the dark. First, grate the Brie over a small camping stool. Slice the other cheeses into small strips, ensuring that you take the Parmesan by surprise. Introducing the Brie at the last minute (unless you are very familiar with this dish, surnames will suffice), fold the cheeses together, taking care to smooth out all the creases with the heel of your foot. Form this mixture into two-inch balls, dust with flour and place them behind the baulk line on the billiard table (ignore the six 'spots': these are for a potted shrimp recipe). Check that there are no more than four balls in the 'D' and then toast them all to a rich brown with the blowtorch. Having allowed the cheese to cool, sprinkle hundreds and thousands liberally over the table's cushions, take the two sticks of celery and, alternating with your companion, try to pot all the pieces of cheese. When there is no cheese left on the table, eat the crisps.

DYNAMITE FLAMBÉ

3 sticks dynamite
1 cup brandy
1 roll masking-tape
1 pr motoring-goggles

Slice the sticks of dynamite into quarter-inch cylinders and arrange attractively around an oval meat-platter. Go into the dining-room and, as surreptitiously as possible so as not to alarm your guests, stick the tape in X-shapes on all the window panes. Return to the kitchen with a tinkling laugh, warm the brandy in a small pan and pour it over the dynamite. Just before you return to your dinner party, put on the goggles and strike a match to ignite the brandy as you re-enter the room.

LEMMING CAKE

1 lemming
6 oz self-raising flour
6 oz margarine
8 oz castor or soft brown sugar
2 large eggs

Challenge the eggs to a fifty-yard race and romp home by a country mile. Once they are thoroughly beaten, whisk them into the flour and margarine. Now melt the lemming with the sugar in a small saucepan, add to the mixture and bake for thirty minutes. Allow the cake to cool on your worktops. Now arrange plates on the floor of the kitchen and wait for the cakes to jump onto them.

SCOTT'S OATES

1 small tent
1 sleeping-bag
1 pen
1 sheet writing-paper

Pitch the tent in your garden and place the sleeping-bag inside so that it looks as though it has been recently vacated. Ensuring that the flap of the tent is hanging loosely and forlornly, leave an enigmatic note to the effect that you will be going out and may be some time. Go and stay with your aunt for a fortnight.

SPOTTED DICK

1 telescope
1 pr binoculars
1 camera with zoom lens

Using the Yellow Pages, discover the whereabouts of your nearest private-detective agency. Rent a room across the street, install your optical equipment and, with the curtains discreetly drawn, sit and wait for one of the detectives to appear. Once you have seen and photographed this occurrence for your archives, celebrate by going out for a meal.

FRUITS DE MER

1 apple
1 pear
1 plum
1 damson
1 mulberry
1 loganberry
1 raspberry
1 strawberry
1 peach
1 orange
1 apricot
8 pts salt water

Put all the fruit in a large bowl, peeling and slicing where necessary. Add the water.

KNICKERBOCKER GLORY

1 pr pants (large)
6 oz chocolate ice-cream
1 leek
1 oz flaked almonds
6 oz cod (filleted)
3 fl oz Kummel

Fill your pants with chocolate ice-cream, add a leek and sprinkle the almonds over them. Now add the cod (I always use this fish, but any bottom-feeder will do). Splash with the Kummel and serve chilled.

Ideal to have after Trouser Risotto (see p64).

MICE PUDDING

4 oz Cheddar cheese
6 mice
3 ins hickory twig
2 oz chicory
2 dock leaves
12 oz ratatouille (which you made earlier)

Holding it with the tail away from you, prepare each mouse by sliding it across your worktops whilst clicking its bottom with your forefinger. Now melt the cheese in a saucepan and lower the mice into it. Allow the mixture to cook until it starts to bubble and squeak. Add the hickory, chicory, dock and turn to a low heat to simmer for half an hour (if you wish you can throw in a little exercise-wheel here to prevent the mice from turning sour) and then allow to cool. When the pudding has solidified, turn it out of the pot, slice thinly and add a helping of ratatouille. Allow your cat to pat each dish across the table to your guests.

Serves 6 (but you might eek it out to 8).

APPLES & PEARS

1 duck
1 Alf garni
2 oz coffee
1 half-inch salt
1 loaf brown bread
syrup of figs

Love the duck and place it on your stairs. Add the bag of herbs and the coffee (I should cocoa the recipe if you have no coffee). Season and leave for as long as you think is reasonable. Use your loaf. Serve on old china with brown bread and chalfonts of syrup. If you think that this recipe lacks credibility, refer to the first two characters mentioned in the book of Genesis.

LAST MANGO IN PARIS

1 mango
8 oz Brando butter
1 lb plaster of Paris

Peel and pip the mango. Mix the plaster with water until you have a thick paste. Now cover the mango in the paste and allow to set. When set, coat with the brando butter and use as a suppository.

VIII. LIQUIDS

EGG TEA

1 egg

Place the egg in a cup or mug. Fill up with boiling water. Leave for two to six minutes, depending on whether you like your eggs hard- or soft-boiled. Remove the egg and dispose of responsibly. Add milk and sugar to taste.

If you decide to make a pot of tea, remember the old adage: 'one egg for each person and one for the pot'. This drink is sometimes known as Ova-ltine.

BLOODY MIRACLE

5 loaves
2 fishes
tomato juice

Assemble a crowd of hungry people and distribute them in a circle around a small hillock. Take the ingredients to the top of the hillock and, without warning, throw everything into the air. Slip away quietly and let them fight it out for themselves.

Serves 5,000.

SLOW GIN

1 dozen snails
1 litre gin
1 lb icing sugar

Pour the gin into a large wide-necked jar (fresh gin is always best and can be caught by setting the usual traps in your garden). Add all the snails and the sugar and then stab the snails over and over again with knitting-needles until they give up. Seal the jar and leave to steep for about three months on the slope behind the coach house. Strain into bottles through a camouflaged tarpaulin, which may not be easy to find. Drink with time to savour. Not to be slugged back.

BRANDY SNAPS

1 bottle Cognac
1 bottle Armagnac
1 bottle Calvados
1 single-lens reflex camera

Put the bottles into all sorts of interesting positions and contexts. Photograph them.

CHAMPAGNE COCKTAILS

4 cockerels
1 bottle vintage Krug Champagne

Nail the cockerels to your worktops, ensuring that they are facing the wall. Shake the bottle vigorously and then uncork it. Immediately thrust the foaming neck of the bottle up the rear of each cockerel in turn. Seal each rear with time-delay window putty. Now retire to a safe distance before the whole thing blows. Have a small sherry at your local inn.

COD'S WALLOP

2 large cod
3 oz brewer's yeast
2 lbs sugar
1 gall water

Bone and skin the cod. Boil all the ingredients except the yeast for one hour. Strain*, cool and add the yeast. Leave in a covered container in a warm room for three days. Strain again and siphon into bottles. Take them to bring-a-bottle parties, put them on the table with all the other contributions and drink something else.

*Dixon's Patent Underpant Strainer is recommended.

CHAMPAGNE COBBLER

1 tspn strained lemon juice
1 tspn orange brandy
Champagne
1 slice of orange
1 lamb's testicle

Put the lemon juice and orange brandy into a tumbler. Add a little ice and fill with the Champagne. Stir gently, drop in the testicle and decorate with a slice of orange. (Vegetarians can substitute nuts for the lamb's testicle.)

EGG FLIP

1 dozen eggs
1 bottle Scotch whisky

Drink the whole of the bottle. Now go into the back garden and, using a soup-spoon, flip all the eggs, one after the other, against the wall of your neighbour's house. Stay in for the rest of the day and on no account answer the door.

BEER SWEETIE

1 pt beer
2 oz sugar

If your maiden aunt expresses a desire for a drink, go into the kitchen, mix the ingredients and take it out to her.

 101

BUCK'S FIZZ

1 male antelope
16 lbs lemon sherbet
1 piping bag
8 pts water
1 trap and harness
1 pr swimming-goggles
1 Sou'Wester

Place the harness on the antelope and position the trap behind it. Taking the piping bag, force the sherbet into the mouth of the antelope followed by the water. Immediately don your protective clothing, sit in the trap and take up the reins. After a few seconds the ingredients in the antelope's stomach will begin their violent reaction and you will start to be propelled forward at great speed. This is a very economical way to do your weekly shop. Be sure to take enough fuel for the journey home.

MILK SHAKE

1 pt milk

Pick up the bottle or carton in one hand, ensuring that it is well sealed. Now move your arm up and down rapidly whilst rotating your wrist from left to right and back again. Do this continuously for at least a minute. When this process has been completed, put the milk into the refridgerator.

CHERRY AID

1 bowl cherries

Pick through the contents of the bowl until you find a cherry which is going through something of a personal crisis and cannot see any light in the darkness of the desperate emotional trough within which it finds itself. Do what you can to help.

STOCKADE

bones from your roasts
1 soda siphon

Make stock in the usual way. When cool, pour into the soda siphon, tighten the top and inject with CO_2 from a gas bulb. Serve in Champagne glasses.

SWIFT HALF

1 swift

Take a sharp knife and slice the bird, from head to tail, in two. Save one piece for later. Grill for ten minutes, turning once. Liquidise and serve on ice.

IX. BRIEFS

CONGA EEL

8 eels

Tie the eels end to end. Now, to the sound of an excruciatingly jolly popular song, force your guests to drag them round the room in time to the music.

FLYING FISH

2 flying fish

Land the fish. Place it in a radical oven. When the fish start to rise, serve immediately.

MOUSSAKA

1 elk

Ask the animal its name. Change it by deed poll.

DOUBLE-HOLLANDAISE SAUCE

2 oz pndjeuuh
5 oz xccvjggf
2 lbs ghhb-jdders
6 yhahihgugfs

Chhj rygf ohgg fiy tggfd iyhh. Ejoigt idfg srrrm ahfff cgtt. Odbjal mghgh pkssbe lvgviiil ehjltd tugitdf. Ehszf cgff unmjky nliy tglwh!!

FRENCH DRESSING

1 beret
1 hooped jumper
1 string onions
1 pr fishnet stockings
20 Gauloise cigarettes
1 lamppost

Put on all the clothes and place the onions around your neck. Now light a cigarette and lean against the lamppost after dark. Inquire as to whether anybody in the vicinity is looking for a good time.

SIX-FRUIT SUMMER PUDDING

6 apples

Peel and core the apples. Eat them.

DOUGHNUTS

30 walnuts
30 pound coins

Mix the ingredients together and serve cold with a receipt.

MARIE ANTOINETTE CAKE

1 Eccles cake
24,653 starving Frenchmen

Set the cake before the Frenchmen. Let them eat it, or have it, but not both.

TZATZIKI

Mix this until you get a word.

MULLED DOVER SOUL

Sit quietly and try to find out the meaning of it all.

SHORT PASTRY

Roll the pastry into a long two-inch wide strip. Now cut it into lots of half-inch lengths. Bake and serve as an *hors d'oeuvre*.

X. FINALLY

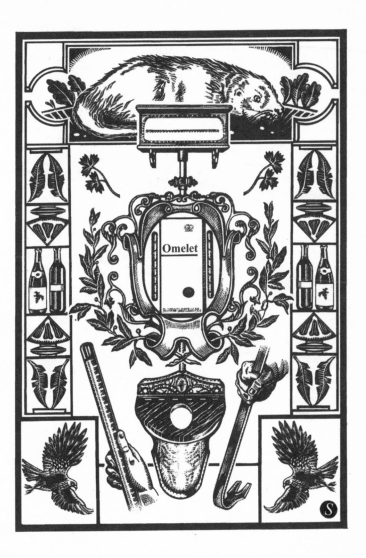

ART IS UNIVERSAL

In my salad days, when I was a young trainee chef, the tricks of the trade were jealously guarded by the established practitioners so that I could only learn by my own mistakes. My goodness how they laughed at my inexperience and naivety, particularly when I took a sledgehammer to a nut and attempted to peel an otter with a spoon. I was even unaware that it was considered bad practice to make gravy from hay! At my cookery school we take pains to see that this Schadenfreude is eradicated by passing on as much as we can. The following is a sample of this advice.

* Never prepare food if your hands are covered in molten lead – it is very poisonous.
* Carrying eggs whilst hopping is asking for trouble.
* It is unwise to put your cat down into a hot frying-pan.
* Fresh ginger should always be grated *before* cooking.
* Keep your hamster away from your tea-bags, otherwise confusion may occur.
* Never keep cockroaches in your sugar bowl.
* Cover the kitchen floor with sawdust to soak up any blood.
* Do not keep brass monkeys in the freezer.
* If your chip-pan catches fire, on no account attempt to put it out with petrol.
* Water salt regularly to prevent it from drying out.
* Try not to store your lemmings near a first-floor window.
* Ensure that the temperature of your fridge is kept well below boiling point.
* After use, keep your kitchen utensils in a bowl of nitric acid.
* If the food in your larder starts to smell, put a clothes-peg on your nose.
* Keep voles in an airtight tin.
* If anything in your fridge has passed its sell-by date, stay on the right side of the law by giving it away.
* Fresh milk should be consumed within eight years of purchase.

X. FINALLY

* *Remember*: some people are allergic to cyanide.
* Never put the dining-room table in the dishwasher.
* It is usually best not to turn the oven on just before going on holiday.
* Never chop peas with a circular saw.
* Before starting to prepare food, ensure that all your work surfaces are free of barbed wire.
* Never put hand-grenades in the microwave.
* If you accidentally chop off a finger, don't waste it. Keep it for making stock.
* Keep flour fresh by tying up the end of the bag with a worm.
* Used cat-litter makes an excellent base for pizza.
* Chicken bones can be sprayed with gold paint and hung from your tree at Christmas.
* Save the fat from your grill-pan to use as bath oil.
* If you need to refer to a particular recipe in this book, use a slug as a bookmark.
* Keep chicken giblets to stuff your pillows.
* If you are sweltering over a stove in hot weather, keep cool by using an apron made from cricket-netting.
* Keep your knives sharp by banging the edge with a hammer.
* White pepper can be stored up your nose.
* Ice cubes are best kept at room temperature.
* After peeling bananas, keep the skins on the floor just inside the front door.
* Keep a piece of kipper in a jar of castor sugar to give it a wonderful perfume.
* Cover your work surfaces with cement to protect them from cuts and scratches.
* To ensure that your kitchen remains clear of smoke, fumes and smells, fit a Rolls-Royce RB211 jet-engine in an outside wall.
* Ensure that all electrical sockets and switches are within easy reach of the sink.
* Always use a sundial to time boiled eggs accurately.
* Save your egg whites in a basket.
* In warm weather, stand sugar lumps in cold water.

A CAUTIONARY TALE

I was once preparing a Vole Supper for the Archduke of Latvia, when I found myself without a vole-wrench and, as a result, the meal was ruined and a diplomatic incident only narrowly avoided. From that day on I swore that my kitchen would be fully equipped at all times. I therefore list here some items without which you, too, might find yourself high and dry.

Aluminium Foil: much safer than a steel épée.
Boxing Glove: needed to make a good punch.
Chelsea Flour: show this to your guests.
Chick Pees: essential for Cock-a-leekie soup
Colander: useful for storing dates.
Crowbar: helps you to break into hen-houses.
Cuckoo Spit: the only way to roast a cuckoo.
Deep Fat Friar: a large monk with an aqualung is always useful.
Egg Poacher: also useful for procuring rabbits, pheasants, deer, etc.
Electric iron: required for any trouser-based recipe.
Electric razor: vital for Eggs Benedictine.
French Bread: this is a pain to make.
French Toast: cheers, *mes amies*!
Fur: Burgers are tasteless without it.
Gin Traps: to ensure a ready supply of gin.
Hand-grater: for when there is absolutely no other food in the larder.
Instant Water Powder: just in case.
Jelly Mould: this can usually be scraped off with a flat knife.
Kitchen Scales: while away those dull moments while dishes are cooking by wheeling the piano into the kitchen.
Lavatory Paper: for basic convenience food.
Lemon-squeezer: actually any Roman emperor will do.

Mandoline: see kitchen scales.
Measuring Spoons: a pointless exercise.
Piping Bag: she is an absolute must for Hogmanay parties.
Ring Mould: this can also be scraped off (carefully) with a flat knife.
Roasting Tin: another pointless exercise.
Rotary Beater: also known as a Mason thrasher.
Rubber Spatula: to make sure it doesn't bend, *au* Geller.
Self-raising Flour: puts itself back on the shelf after use.
Serving Spoon: less effective than a tennis racquet.
Sledgehammer: useful for tenderising large cuts of meat.
Slotted Spoon: useless for soup.
Spam Javelin: *la crème de la crème* of skewers.
Sugar Tongs: good, but tend to dissolve in hot dishes.
Thermometer: to assist in curing haddock.
Tramp-steamer: for tenderness in any vagrant-based dishes.
Vegetable Chopper: this complements the existing animal and mineral versions.
Wheat Beer: keep in stock for thirsty Frenchmen.

At some stage you may also need the following:
Claw Hammer, Trowel, Dustbins, Surgeon's Saw, Matches, Electric Whisk, Quiz Book, Fire-extinguisher, Billiard Cues, Window Putty, Knitting Needles, Camouflaged Tarpaulin, Milk Brush, Elastic Bands, Electric Toaster, Ice-cream Scoop, Pot Stands, Vole-wrench, Pile-tweezers, Haggis-tongs.

ACKNOWLEDGEMENTS

Where does one start when trying to express gratitude to those who have been of invaluable assistance along the way? The problem lies, not in whom to mention, but in whom to leave out. Tribute has already been paid to my great-aunt Sopwith, but there have been others. My publisher, Mr Croft, a far less odious individual than the afore-mentioned unfortunate with whom I was previously associated, at least, pays some attention to the small matter of personal hygiene. I should here mention, too, in order of ascending unimportance, those whose suggestive behaviour has been greatly valued: Mr Inwood, Madame Skewers and Miss Gillespie. Fulsome praise for similar activity over the years is also due to Messrs Edwards and Northcote-Green. To those remaining that I have unwittingly omitted, I offer my apologies and, nonetheless heartfelt, thanks. Last, but certainly not least, I commend to you Sparks, the draughtsman. Rhino-quills and octopus-ink are seldom used these days, but his insistence on keeping these traditional methods alive does him – and this book – immense credit. Long may he remain a member of my staff, for it is always a pleasure to return his cheery wave as I pass by the gatehouse every morning.

I would also like to thank the following:

Acme Stomach-Pumps Ltd
Armitage Shanks
British Owl Fanciers
David Elizabeth
Equity
H.M. Customs & Habits
Multilever Ltd
Snails 'R' Us
The Cod Council
The Custard Society
The Earwig Association
The Electrical Association for Women
The Fire Brigade
The Geriatric Nutrition Unit
The Gooseberry Information Bureau
The Kipper Club
The Ministry of Food
The Orange-peel Research Council
The Otter Board
The Squirrel Society
The Royal Alimentary Hospital
The Royal Society for the Protection of Prawns
United Trousers Ltd
Vole-u-Like

The ensuing pages contain some of the notices
printed in the original edition of First, Peel the Otter.

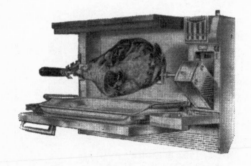

*

DIXON'S PATENT
MULTIFARIOUS EGG-TIMER

*

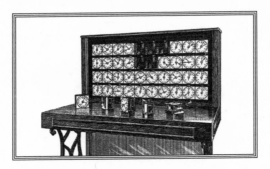

MOST EFFICACIOUS
FOR BREAKFAST SITTINGS OF UP TO
FORTY PEOPLE

THE VARIOUS AND DIFFERING
REQUIREMENTS OF INDIVIDUALS MAY BE
EASILY ACCOMMODATED WITH THIS
MODERN EQUIPMENT.

BY ROYAL LETTERS PATENT

DIXON'S PATENT
LEMMING JUICE

THERE IS NONE *TANGIER*

PREPARED FROM RIPE LEMMINGS PERSONALLY
SELECTED AND SQUEEZED BY MR JOHN HENRY DIXON

BY ROYAL LETTERS PATENT

DIXON'S PATENT
TABBYASCO SAUCE

'THE *PURRFECT* SAUCE'

SPECIALLY SUITED FOR PURPOSES WHERE
PIQUANCY IS REQUIRED

*

DIXON'S PATENT
UNDERPANT STRAINER

*

MOST INDISPENSABLE FOR
THE REMOVAL OF ANTS FROM
YOUR SAUCES

WITH *EASILY CLEANABLE* GUSSET,
REMOVABLE WINGED FILTERS AND
FULLY ELASTICATED RIM

*

DIXON'S PATENT
POWDERED DODO EGG

*

NO SIFTING REQUIRED

MAY BE BOILED, CODDLED, FRIED, POACHED OR SCRAMBLED
WITH THE SIMPLE ADDITION OF WATER

'FOR THE *RAREST* OF FEASTS'

AVAILABLE WHILST STOCKS LAST

*

DIXON'S PATENT
KITCHEN TROUSER-PRESS

*

'IT MAY DO TO FOLD IN BUTTER,
BUT TROUSERS ARE QUITE A DIFFERENT
KETTLE OF FISH.'

FOR A *CREASE-FREE* RISOTTO

ADDITIONAL **SLEEVE-BOARD** ALSO AVAILABLE

*

DIXON'S PATENT
STEAM-DRIVEN
FIG-SORTER

*

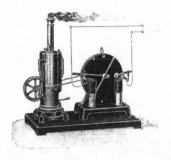

THIS WONDROUS AND MAGICAL MACHINE
WILL TRANSMOGRIFY THE TEDIUM OF
SELECTING **THE GOOD FRUIT** (*SEE FIG. 1*)
AND DISCARDING **THE BAD** (*SEE FIG. 2*)
INTO A PLEASURE.

Fig. 1   Fig. 2

JOHN HENRY DIXON'S UTENSIL EXCHANGE

PART-EXCHANGE SERVICE TO COOKERY STUDENTS

OLD POTS EXCHANGED FOR *NEW* AT
VERY REASONABLE PRICES

CONTACT THE SERJEANT-AT-ARMS AT

JOHN HENRY DIXON'S SCHOOL OF COOKERY

JOHN HENRY DIXON'S SCHOOL OF COOKERY

THE LARGEST AND MOST SUCCESSFUL OF ITS KIND IN THE WORLD

120 CARBON STREET, BLACKBURN

FOR IMPROVEMENT IN DOMESTIC CAPABILITIES

CLASSES PERSONALLY CONDUCTED BY MR JOHN HENRY DIXON, DAILY, EXCEPT SATURDAYS, 10.30 A.M. TO ABOUT 4.00 P.M.
(LUNCHEON: NOON UNTIL 3.00 P.M.)

CULINARY LESSONS GIVEN IN: ARM-PITTING, BLOOD-CURDLING, CARROT-TOPPING, COD-BATTERING, CORN-FLAKING, DOG-EARING, EARL-FOLDING, EARWIG-GUTTING, FREEZE-GRILLING, HAND TOSSING, HEDGEHOG-PRICKING, HORSE-WHIPPING, ICE-ROASTING, LAMB-BASTING, LEG-SPREADING, MUSSEL-BUILDING, NUT-TIGHTENING, ONION-BARGING, ORANGE-SQUASHING, OTTER-PEELING, OVEN-FREEZING, PARROT-FASHIONING, POT-JOINTING, SPIT-DRIZZLING, STOCK-RUSTLING, TEETH-GRATING, TORTOISE-SHELLING, TRAMP-STEAMING, WHELK-FLATTENING AND OTHER BASIC KITCHEN PROCEDURES.

INSTRUCTION IN PROCUREMENT COVERS: ANT-SHOOTING, BEAN-STALKING, BEET-NICKING, BEE-GETTING, BUFFALO-DODGING, CABBAGE-HUNTING, CANDLE-STICKING, CLARET-DRILLING, COCOA-NUTTING, DOG-BADGERING, EEL-FEELING, EGG-POACHING, FLY-FISHING, FROG-LEAPING, GIRAFFE-TOPPLING, GIN-TRAPPING, HEAD-SPINNING, HERB-SNARING, LARK-DIGGING, LETTUCE-PREYING, MOLE-WRENCHING, MOOSE-NOOSING, MOTH-GATHERING, OWL-FISHING, PANCAKE-LANDING, PEAR-TRAWLING, PLASTER-CASTING, SHEIKH-SPEARING, SHEEP-REARING, SLUG-CHASING, SNAIL-TRACKING, SOLE-SEARCHING, TOAD-HAULING, TROUT-TICKLING AND VOLE-STRANGLING.

FURTHER TRAINING AVAILABLE IN: BEAVER-SPLITTING, BITCH-COMBING, BOMB-AIMING, CHICKEN-JUGGLING, FEATHER-DUSTING, FOWL-SMELLING, FRENCH DRESSING, GOAT-COUNSELLING, HARE-SPLITTING, HEART-RENDING, MULBERRY-HARBOURING, MOP-ROLLING, OAK-MINDING, OWL-FANCYING, PIGEON-HOLING, PLAICE-SETTING, PORRIDGE-SERVING, ROCKET-SCIENCE, RUM-AGEING, SAUSAGE-HIDING, SHEEP-WORRYING AND WORM-BLENDING. MORSE CODE, AND SLEEP-DEPRIVATION TECHNIQUES ALSO TAUGHT.

WE ALSO FIND OURSELVES IN A POSITION TO PROVIDE:-
HIRE: FOR SUPPLYING, ON A TEMPORARY BASIS, EQUIPMENT TO EXPEDITE YOUR PREPARATORY ACTIVITIES.
GOODS: A FIRST-CLASS RANGE OF KITCHEN EQUIPMENT AND REQUISITES. PLEASE APPLY FOR A FULL LIST OF
DIXON'S PATENT EQUIPMENT AND REQUISITES.

ESTIMATES GIVEN FREE FOR THE ENTIRE FURNISHING OF KITCHENS IN ACCORDANCE WITH THE REQUIREMENTS OF

MODERN COOKERY

OTHER BOOKS BY JOHN HENRY DIXON

Sadly, all of these titles are long out of print.

Cookery

Cooking Underground – The Secret Diary of a Mole
Starters for Beginners
Cramped Cookery – Easy Meals for Bomber Crews
Cooking with Lead
Salad Daze – The Side-effects of Vegetarianism
Broth Cooking for Multiple Chefs
Dodo – The Missing Ingredient
Devour a Whale in Eighty Days
Living with Botulism
Let the Cockroach be Your Friend
Waist Disposal – The Nuneaton Diet
The Slug and Your Kitchen
Salmonella – The Way Forward
A Man for All Seasons
The Watercress File
Tinker, Tailor, Soldier, Chef
Seven Pillars of Salt
All Creatures Taste Great
Madame Bovril

Other Subjects

Scale Models of Fish
Catch Twenty-Two Fish